I
ENCOURAGE
YOU TO
LIVE

Volume One

Skye David

authorHOUSE®

AuthorHouse™
1663 Liberty Drive
Bloomington, IN 47403
www.authorhouse.com
Phone: 1 (800) 839-8640

Published by AuthorHouse 08/01/2019

ISBN: 978-1-7283-1310-8 (sc)
ISBN: 978-1-7283-1309-2 (e)

Library of Congress Control Number: 2019906349

Print information available on the last page.

Any people depicted in stock imagery provided by Getty Images are models, and such images are being used for illustrative purposes only. Certain stock imagery © Getty Images.

This book is printed on acid-free paper.

DEDICATIONS

I dedicate this series to the game changers of my life.
To my sons Alex and Ryan, you both have caused so much needed
change in my life. I am forever thankful to God to have the both of you
as my children; wonderful blessings that I love and cherish dearly.
Apostle Hines thank you for being the father I never had,
because you have been the one person I always trust.
Prophetess Hines thank you for continually pushing me because
this has caused growth and helped shape my character.

ACKNOWLEDGEMENTS

I give the greatest acknowledgement to God who is everything to my life. I want to acknowledge the work of my spiritual mother, Prophetess Audra L Hines. Thank you for being my continual encouragement during the many attempts that I tried to stop writing this series. This book was written through personal experiences to understand God's intent on each subject and you made some of those sacrifices with me on this journey. I appreciate the time you have put in to the progress of this series. You have a busy life and you still made time to attend focus meetings. Mom, thank you for challenging me to expand the content of the I Encourage You to Live series when I wanted to limit it to a small, simple book to avoid the painful experiences that were paired with every chapter. Writing this book at full length and intent from God I have gained spiritual maturity.

Thank you to my spiritual father, Apostle Kelvin E. Hines Sr., because you have spoken and declared God's purpose in to my life when I did not see what I was worth you saw me in the eyes of God.

Thank you sincerely to my sisters Pastor Marjorie Patino, Elder Jamecka McLean and Aisha Littles for your prayers were always felt in the midst of my pain. Thank you to Elder Cytrilla Mitchell because you gave me the biggest push to get back into ministry when you spoke obedience back into my soul. A special thank you to my sister Stayzha Lee for being a place of unconditional love while

I was grieving. Thank you for the battles you faced first and then encouraged me to smile in spite of everything that I suffered through. To my sister Rebekah Arthur, you have stood as confirmation and testimony of the words God has placed in my heart.

FOREWORD

In life one of the very first songs we learn is our ABC's song. Making sure the rhythm is just right every letter pronounced perfectly latticed. Everyone know how excited we were that our precious child has learned her ABC's, letting her sing them to all who would listen. As we mature day by day, year by year, our ABC's get distorted. Life leads to journeys seen and unseen, wanted and unwanted that simple song is somehow changed to Murmurs and Complaints A to Z. No longer a happy song for many. In the eye of the storm Amber has found her ABC song again finding herself in each alphabet with strong faith choosing to encourage others with her life from A to Z. In her intimate time with God hearing who he created her to be, being a living breathing testimony striving each day to be better has chosen to encourage others. Raising her hand shouting I'll be the example the example from A to Z. your story may not be her story however this story is for sure one to know knowing that God's grace is sufficient. You may never sing her ABC's again but you're Living Life A to Z. Be encouraged my sister, my brother.

Finish Strong.
Prophetess Audra Hines

Introduction

All scriptures are given from the Amplified Version of the Holy Bible. The <u>I Encourage You to Live</u> series is intended to be very easy to read. Volume one focuses on the key concepts in: awakening as spiritual birth, understanding the value of blessings, positioning with true compassion to birth life in others, living as a genuine disciple of God, accepting that God is everlasting, the freedom from bondage that happens with forgiveness and the importance of knowing the true purpose of grace. The <u>I Encourage You to Live</u> series is everything you need to thrive spiritually from A to Z. The use of first and second person writing is intentional because it is a personal uplifting of the soul and no matter where God positions is, we all are subject to God's will. You will notice that some lists can be very lengthy and this is done so that there are no assumptions about the multitude of problems that can arise. Every section in this volume has a personal testimony. I warm you that some testimonies are graphic and vivid as I wanted to be absolutely transparent about all experiences and circumstances I faced. I did this because it allows people to realize that anyone can be used to do God's will and even in low, dark and shameful moments everyone deserves an abundant life. I speak life to you and I encourage you to live a life of increase.

CONTENTS

AWAKENING

L<small>ORD, WE GIVE REVERENCE</small> to Your name, we honor You as our Father and thank You for heavenly inheritance. We welcome You in our lives to shine in us, so You see Your name be glorified. Lord, let Your will be done in us. Lord, we put away our agendas and come from a place of submission and eagerness to be living examples of what You have purposed. Thank you, Lord, for the Bible because it is Your word of truth, salvation, and deliverance. God, help us to live in Your Word daily that it may edify us; so that we are sustained and will not want to eat trash. Please help us receive the knowledge and the power of the Word, and the impact of activating who we are destined to be in as people in Your kingdom. Please allow Your spirit to manifest in us so we may prosper, and not just physically, but in our souls. We thank you for giving us the opportunity to change. Let us know we are Your children and we are new people within You. Speak life into Your children Father, and let us awaken the untapped blessings that come from living in You.

In the name of Jesus, I command what has held us captive will be loosed, and God's children receive every blessing in this manual. Our minds will no longer give audience to curses, and our hearts will no longer be tormented with the affliction of demonic spirits. We command the authority of God to take who we know ourselves to be and cause it to flee so that we can be who You called us to be in purpose. Amen.

"But everything exposed by the light becomes visible–and everything that is illuminated becomes a light. Therefore, it is said: 'Wake up, sleeper, rise from the dead, and Christ will shine on you.'" (Ephesians 5:13-14). This is the proper way to start every day as you awaken to face the battle life is going to bring against your soul.

I ask you to open your heart to this book and allow this message to overtake you spiritually. Why? Because you are about to fight the devil all day. Be open to understanding that this is not another "self-help" book because this is a God Help manual. To comprehend who we are, we first must wake up.

How do you wake up? This scripture is so powerful as it calls the dead back to life. It is spoken that you must wake up that Christ may shine in you. To do this, you must turn away from everything that represents death in your life. When you live in something for a long time, you may not even recognize it as death.

Look at the secular couple founded on the principle of lust. This couple will say that they love each other, but on the inside do not find any truth in the relationship. This couple does not speak to their partner with respect and may make excuses for the faults of their bond together. True love should cover all faults in this pairing and find ways to alter hateful situations. This couple lasted about three months from start to finish and could only agree to lay down with each other. They were so comfortable pleasing their flesh, not understanding that the relationship was dead because it produced nothing of life to those participating.

The first step to *awakening* your new vision is to give your life to Christ; accepting Jesus as your Lord and Savior will be the start of your new life. You become aware when you have accepted the truth that Jesus conquered death so that His children will never have to die again. Your eyes are now open to see the dead things in your surroundings. Like a baby, when you first open your eyes, some things will appear blurry. Your situation will be seen in just black and white. The good thing is that the longer your eyes stay open, the more your vision becomes clear and vivid.

The second step is to study the Bible passionately. Know that studying is not as simple as just reading the Word; studying means to get into the Word and grasp its meaning. Surface reading is not enough to keep you from returning to a thought process of death, but instead, you must meditate and pray until there is clarity. Pray and ask God to give you spiritual guidance so that it can resonate in your soul.

The third step is to walk by divine instruction. That means that you need to understand what God has asked of you and where you are placed in the kingdom. John 15:16, declares, "You have not chosen me, but I have chosen you and I have appointed and placed and purposefully planted you, so that you would go and bear fruit and keep on bearing." Learn how to spread the Gospel and bring others to freedom by knowing Jesus as their Savior.

You will start to function with true sight in the Lord. Your eyes are open wide, and you will see that some people carry death with them, and you will notice the curses that have come to attack you. A common curse is the curse of division. The curse of division brings its friends bitterness, anger, restlessness, and many more curses to spread chaos and bondage. It is Satan's concern that he shows his face to steal from, kill off and destroy your growth and divisional curses are a form of this destruction. James 1:8 says, "A double-minded man is unstable and restless in all his ways in everything he thinks, feels, or decides." Therefore, most divisional curse can be attached to an emotion, especially in important bonds and connections that have a divine purpose. In today's generation, there is division running wild in marriage, and divorce is the product of this curse. The children created from this union may feel that they are not going to be married because their parents did not stay together. It is important to recognize exposure to curses and strengthen your relationship with God so that you can understand that curses, even generational curses, have no hold on your new life.

New sight will also require action. In Genesis 12:1, God tells Abraham to get up and go, because He will lead you and you must be willing to follow. Your heart must be open to what God has in store for you. He will show you that He will take you away from the enemy and will save you from unseen dangers. What is an unseen danger? Today there is now a misconception that the enemy is someone you may not like, but an enemy could present itself as anyone in your life. Your enemy could be a longtime friend who does not accept that you have given your life to God and thinks you should be in the club with them. An enemy could be the sibling that you care about that continues to drag you down with their poor attitude. Because Satan is always around, you will have to stay on the path with God and not stray because Satan will use anyone he can to destroy what God has for you, and kill the future destiny God has purposed for you. Know that your path was not made easy to travel because living clean is a daily battle against your flesh. God will lead you up steep hills, through treacherous mountains and darkening depths, and if you are in line with Him, you are protected on this journey. Use your new eyes to read the rest of this manual to mature in the Lord.

My Testimony

I was always different and made fun of for just being me. I struggled through addictions and bad relationships and started to proclaim death in my life. I woke up drinking, and many times, I prepared a bowl of cereal with White Russians instead of milk. I drank brandy and snorted pain pills on breaks at work. I went back home to change clothes and go out to find random men to lay with each night. I was insatiable with sex and I did not care who I got it from or their circumstance I was only thinking about lust and perversion. I dabbled in witchcraft and I told myself I was only a pair of legs because that is how my history was and this should now be my expectation in life. I exposed my soul to hell and continued because it made me feel invincible. About a decade ago, I met a man who I loved for a few years who ended the relationship wounding me physically and spiritually and I decided to come back to Arizona not too long after the relationship ended. I went to three other churches who knew me as a child, but no one sensed the hell I was living as a functioning alcoholic, hitting the club, always angry, sleeping with a team of men and caring so much less about my life. My children had to suffer through some things that no child should ever be exposed to, and it has caused trauma in their way of thinking. Then I met a man who took me with him to church one day, and I met some angels.

I went up to get prayer, and God spoke to me through my pastors. I knew people were assuming Prophetess was speaking to me about a tattoo on my shoulder, but she was telling me about the demonic tattoo I have on my left leg. They instantly took me in as one of their own children and have never treated me differently to this day! God had bigger plans in store for me. In May 2013, I gave my life to Jesus to begin a journey that I did not prepare for and soon suffered an attack from the devil. In 2015, I told God, "Yes, I'll do what you have called me to do," and I joined the Mime ministry. Later that year in July, I broke my foot in two places while practicing for a song we had to minister that Sunday. The sad thing is that God only did it to put me in my place – a higher place. I had now started to feel what it meant to fast, to depend on people I don't trust even to hold my water, and it opened my eyes to see how many people close to me hated to see what I sacrificed for ministry. God told me that summer to write this book. Each section has brought me through a trial, as God knows it is best to write from experience. There is nothing written here that I have not experienced. It took much longer than what I was told because I tried to shorten what God gave me to say. I also failed so many tests from God, and I could not write until my heart was changed. Some people look at me and do not think that I may understand what it is like to choose death over your children because it was an addictive lifestyle. It took many people to war for the change in my soul, and I am so thankful that God placed people in my life who pushed me. I am so thankful to the people who motivated me, and the people that the devil put in my path because I am stronger for every experience.

BLESSINGS

THE BLESSINGS OF THE Lord are great and incredible to possess.

The Lord manifests His blessings in the natural and in the spiritual presence. In the natural realm, it is so easy to see a blessing, because it is seen as the praise report of a new job or the testimony of closing on a house purchase. Natural or physical blessings can also be seen as a final notice bill paid before shutting off, or a car being purchased as transportation no matter what condition of the vehicle. Did you know that anyone can be blessed in the physical realm? God said in Matthew 5:45 that His sun rises on the good and evil and that His rain falls on the righteous and unrighteous. There is no requirement needed for physical blessings to be released into the atmosphere. Being blessed or receiving blessings in the spiritual presence have a great and more powerful impact because your spirit is forever. After your body is gone, your soul will remain, so you want blessings to flow past what is just done on earth. I know I want us to be blessed long after the earth is gone, and that everlasting blessings rain in your life!

How do you know from where spiritual blessings come? Ephesians 1:3-5 says, "Blessed and worthy of praise be the God and Father of our Lord Jesus Christ, who has blessed us with every spiritual blessing in the heavenly realms in Christ, just as He chose us in Christ before the foundation of the world, so that we would be holy and blameless in His sight. In love He predestined and lovingly planned for us to be adopted to Himself as children through Jesus Christ, in accordance with the kind of intention and good pleasure of His will." The children of God can only obtain spiritual blessings. Now that you are a child of God, and have accepted Him into your heart, you are choosing not to limit your blessings to what is just manifested on earth.

God created you with the plan of showing His face even though He did not need anyone to accept Him. Be excited because God appreciates that you are willing to change to be a new creature and that you know this must be done because adoption is not an easy process. Adoption is the action of officially accepting and approving a new union, bond, or connection that will facilitate growth. Adoption requires an agreement that is considered between a new parent and their new child to care for and nurture the child until maturity. Adoption means that the Lord is now accepting you in because you are giving Him the approval to open you to a new realm of blessings as His child. Adoption requires contract to be signed with and with a contract signed it is a done deal. God does not break His contract and it cannot be undone. God picked you before you were created – the Bible says that even before the foundation of the world, you are chosen to be blessed. That means that you were created to be blessed. God is no respecter of person that if you do not have an earthly title, you cannot be blessed. His only requirement is that you be His son. Now that your eyes are open to the understanding of being a child of God, He can rain down blessings from heavenly realms.

Take a deeper look to see who the people are that God will spiritually bless? The answer is found in Proverbs 28:20, where it is proclaimed that God rains down His blessings on those who are faithful to Him. The children who trust in God as the giver of every provision will be blessed. What does it mean to be faithful? To be faithful is to be unwavering. When you are faithful, you are trusting in God for all needs to be met. You must make the decision that God will only add to your life. Faithful to God and standing firm with expectation and hope, knowing God will give you everything you need. In Proverbs 10:6, we are also told that blessings are on the heads of the righteous who walk upright with God. Blessings are given to His faithful children who walk where God's purpose is fulfilled. That means that you get the understanding that you must stay in the position where you have been placed with God. Let's look at some very awesome blessings now that we understand what is required to activate the inheritance of blessings.

My favorite blessing is found in John 10:28 because Jesus spoke that He has given us eternal life and that His children will never perish or be snatched from His hand. Your soul will live eternally through Christ, which now means that you are now blessed with abundant life here on earth and in heaven. Jesus took all power, so there is nothing that can conquer your Father. This is the beauty of blessings because the living needs to be fed to stay alive, and God will not bless you with life without fulfilling the promise for you to keep living.

Proverbs 10:3 is typically looked at as a promise of a physical blessing, but it has a deeper meaning as a spiritual blessing. In this scripture, God blesses the righteous that they will never hunger. What God is saying is that He has provided for His children, so they are not going to starve or feel the need to feed on garbage. God gave you the Word so that you are continually given all the nourishment your soul needs to stay full in the Lord. God's word covers all questions you have and has been designed by God so that there is no "loophole" to deny you a blessing. God's word will not return to Him void, so use it to keep feeding yourself with knowledge and blessings.

Another life changing blessing is a hidden blessing. What is a hidden blessing? This type of blessing manifests through the trial that is tearing down your flesh to strengthen you and growing your character secretly. Hidden blessings come from the trial that you conquer when you thought all hope was gone. God won every battle and used you to show that there is a victory in every situation that seemed like it was a lost cause. Think of the power of a hidden blessing. The ultimate trial was death, and that was conquered. Jesus was tried and persecuted by the people who claimed to love Him. He was forced to carry His cross, burdened by the weight of the device of His death. His flesh broken as Jesus was beaten to the point He was unrecognizable as a person; and then, all hope seemed to be lost as Christians watched Jesus on display, already impelled by evildoers who showed Him nothing less than hatred. Jesus confronted God with a plea of mercy on behalf of man with His last breath and died. In His death, He went down into hell and snatched the keys of hell and death. He conquered death and lived again, eternally. Look at the power of hidden blessings! Jesus took it all to fulfill a prophecy of blessing. His trial was great, and the world was against Him, yet He spoke into existence the blessing of second chance. God, Father, give the people another opportunity to live and live in freedom. Jesus blessed us by taking authority over death, and the fight has been fixed in your favor. Through Him being your Father, you have everlasting life, and every situation that brings death has already been conquered. You have an amazing opportunity to give your life to God to be blessed above physical comprehension. It does not matter who talks about you or what comes to harm you; God is in control. In this book, many blessings will be addressed so that they can be released into the atmosphere. This will help the next time; you can praise about being blessed with victory over the enemy and not just anytime something physical changes.

My Testimony

Amen – nothing from God comes easy. I had a problem with jealousy toward seeing people being blessed with new things, as I sat around with nothing new. I had lost sight of why I prayed to God to bless me when I realized that He never stopped blessing me. I realized every day I am given a chance to be blessed because I am His son. It was up to me to understand why God had me placed in my situation. It changed what I asked for and my heart toward other people receiving new cars and houses. God showed me that His blessings are everlasting, and I can have access if I choose to tap into spiritual blessings, and I will lose jealousy toward my brothers and sisters; this was bigger than if I got a new purse or clothes. I had to realize I also needed to be in the right place to receive the blessing. I no longer shout for a new car blessing, but I shout about a blessing of wisdom, I pray for inner peace and clarity, and I stopped asking for worldly possessions. I went a year and still have not bought another purse, and I am okay with what I have. I know that if I am doing the will of God, everything my heart desires will come to pass. God if you grant me the insight I will know how to get my new house, God if I follow your word my husband will come, God if I work diligently to seek your face my heart will be full of you, and I will be in the right state of mind. I now surround myself with people who are being blessed with these gifts, and God has lifted my level of insight. I praise God for the people I see being blessed because He is releasing it into the atmosphere. My praise says, "I know God that you are in my zip code and I welcome you to release everything you are right here."

COMPASSION

"Carry one another's burdens, and in this way, you will fulfill the requirements of the law of Christ, that is, the law of Christian love." (Galatians 6:2)

What is compassion? I struggled to gain clarity with embodying compassion and how naïve I was to this concept. God explains compassion as suffering long with something or someone as if their problem were your own. In this section, we are going to be dealing with true suffering so that it is not misunderstood. We will understand that with long-suffering, we must recognize it as a heavy burden, bearing and delivering for others. It is important to the process of victory to understand the impacts of compassion and the value of not confusing it with expressing sympathy.

Compassion is sometimes misconstrued to be showing sympathy. People who have not mastered compassion show assumptions of sympathy, which is very misleading and harmful. To understand compassion, we first must know sympathy and why this should not be conveyed as compassion. Sympathy is acknowledging that someone is in a situation and to apologize for what they are facing in their storm. The problem with sympathy is that there is no ownership displayed. Sympathy is effortless as our minds have been programmed to say, "I'm sorry to hear that," without thought or genuine concern. Sympathy is a learned behavior that has numbed compassion out of today's society. We, as Christians, have the power and authority to abolish all concepts of sympathy because God lives in us. Sympathy is a passive trick of Satan to disguise having compassion through misleading statements. I had always failed to understand why I was supposed to be fake about caring for someone. I did not understand why I was not successful with sympathy until I was twenty-eight years old.

God had to show me why I would not express sympathy correctly when He took me to 1 John 3:18. The first point that was revealed is that God is not fake about compassion. God has never changed His word to allow people to stay ill or reject healing. The second revelation is that words spoken without loving and sincere action is only lip service; talk is cheap and lame words being uttered loosely is ungodly because there is an absence of life being spoken. The third point is that compassion is not expressed without action. God does not change His word, but He does change His presence as an action to protect during the storm. God is living water for good reason because the battle can be fought in different scenarios, and all who stay faithful have the outcome of victory. I must ask that we stop using simple heartless words to assume they can help others through their trials. The trials people are going through are God's way of strengthening and elevating in faith, so there is no reason to be sorry for God working in someone's life. The responsibility we need to take as the body of Christ is to step in and suffer with the person in the heart of the storm.

God wants us to comprehend that to act with compassion is to operate with long-suffering. "Let love of your fellow believers continue. Do not neglect to extend hospitality to strangers (especially among the family of believers—being friendly, cordial, and gracious, sharing the comforts of your home and doing your part generously), for by this some have entertained angels without knowing it. Remember those who are in prison, as if you were their fellow prisoner, and those who are mistreated, since you also are in the body (and subject to physical suffering)." (Hebrews 13:1-3) This is a set of instructions to display compassion, as Jesus showed compassion to the church. In the process of long-suffering, every action you take needs to be made in God's love. You truly must carry love for everyone deep in your heart to suffer with someone. The next part of this scripture was to inform us that when acting with compassion, we must take on the role of the midwife.

In the physical realm, the role of the midwife is to have a successful birth of a child. The midwife carries the same function in the spiritual realm. When a trial presents itself, be aware that God is trying to birth something new and better that is of benefit to that person and glorifies God. Not everyone can handle birth on their own, and this is the importance of the midwife's assignment. The midwife's understanding of birth is labor and delivery, and this comes by being seasoned in prayer. There is always labor before delivery, even if you assume your labor has no pain. A true midwife does not show concern to a name, title, or the past through baring with a person during labor. The midwife embodies confidence because they are mature and experienced; so, you will not find a midwife that is not loud, boastful, or full of pride. The midwife does what is necessary to have a healthy birth. That means that if the labored and heavy burdened need to be comforted, the midwife will comfort to ensure a healthy birth.

Being a compassionate person requires that you express comfort to the suffering. If the afflicted need healing, the midwife assesses the wounds and begins to pray until there is a report of better health. "When He saw the crowds, He was moved with compassion and pity for them, because they were dispirited and distressed, like sheep without a shepherd. Then He said to His disciples, 'The harvest is (indeed) plentiful, but the workers are few. So, pray to the Lord of the harvest to send out workers into His harvest.'" (Matthews 9:36-38) The midwife locks to that person's spirit to assist and share in the labor pains. Is your prayer life strong enough to cry out to God for birth in someone's life, and He hears you? Labor pains are a form of suffering that is a torment to take your mind to dark places, can have you step out of character, create doubt in your ability to birth and open doors to emotional chaos that has the potential to abort what needs to be birthed. The midwife holds your hand in encouragement to keep you calm in labor and to remember the goal of a successful birth. Labor is rough, and delivery is a place of freedom and sometimes a stronger attack. This is to help give strength when you feel weak, to uplift you when you feel low, to bring clarity when your mind is clouded, to hold your pain when you are about to lose your mind and to tell you that delivery time is coming. God delivers when he has determined that labor is done and that it is time to push! It is now time for what is inside of you to come forth and live.

Satan has a clear understanding of God's presence and working knowledge of the freedom he lost when he stood against God and was cast out of heaven. This is where it gets dangerous, as any false move can cause death or birth defects. This is where it gets tougher than labor because delivery requires that there be pushing. Push! Push past the attack, because the birth is worth everything to that person's new life. Push against the attack, know how to proclaim God to the attack, and live. Be the midwife that says to keep going it's almost over. Then the deliverance is here, and everyone can see them victorious, full of new life, a remarkable sight. Deliverance has brought forth something better in them that God's glory shines brighter for everyone to take witness of transformation.

I encourage you to live and live strong enough to stand in the gap for those who are transforming. A prayer life is a key to achieving compassion and watching our sisters and brothers in Christ rise up strong and victorious!

My Testimony

I watched a family member deal with a very hard and horrific situation. I was there for them in the beginning, not knowing that I would be presented the same storm a few months later. I used to bring them money and food to help because I thought that was showing compassion to others – I was so wrong, as I watched the sacrifices I was making being abused to let someone continue to make poor choices. I had to change and find compassion in my heart and stop throwing money at a problem that was not getting fixed. I encouraged them to live, and they chose to keep speaking death into their situation. I realized that what I was doing wasn't compassion, and I was enabling them to continue making poor decisions that were going to end in destruction. I started praying for a change in their soul and that a horrific situation be turned to activate what God has planned. I had to step back and realize that I was in the way of them discovering birth and that I can stand by them (whether they feel it or not) till change comes. When I stepped into my own storm, I felt a difference at the beginning of my situation, and God placed a few midwives for me. I felt their prayers for victory, and for God to completely heal me. See their prayers were on my behalf, and God is working to change my heart for His glory. I knew I had to stand in the gap for someone else, and it was going to be up to me to be obedient to God to be used to change someone else's life.

DISCIPLESHIP

DISCIPLESHIP IS THE GREAT dying to yourself and the divorcing from the flesh. There is so much reward in true discipleship that the Lord looks to release and increase in your life. Being a true disciple is so important that God wants to make sure that we understand what it means to be a disciple of Jesus Christ and the value of discipleship.

Discipleship is based on your understanding with full comprehension of the value of divorce and the death that you will face. You will have to divorce your old husband of wickedness and cling to your new husband for your dear life. To do this, you must understand that there are now two contracts signed on your life as one is toward everlasting life and one is of the destruction that Satan drafts to bring death to your decision of abundant life. Your first contract is to Jesus as we find in Ephesians 5:23-24, He is the husband to the church. Jesus has a few requirements in your marriage contract that must be actively maintained. One of these requirements is divorcing the husband of your flesh. That means that you must kill off the old you or it will suffocate and consume your ability to function as a wife in your marriage to Christ. This is the process of dying to your deep-rooted sinful desires, mindsets, relationships, and poor choices. You must be willing to take Godly council until you bury your old way of thinking. It is mandatory that you continually study the Word of God, pray for guidance, and discern the advice of righteous people. Bury the voice that tells you to do something to hurt others and actions that you will end up regretting once it is done. You will find your strength and wisdom in Jesus that is why it is important to cling to Him, making your union stronger. Your husband is going to be everything you will ever need for the rest of your life. You must remember His protection is vital to keep you from being harmed by the second contract on your life.

Satan signs the second contract against you because he wants to kill and destroy your marriage to Jesus. This is not the time to panic, but this is when you begin to fight for your marriage. See Satan was your old husband, and now that you are married to the King, his feelings are hurt. When there are hurt feelings and bruised egos, there is a malicious attack because there is jealousy displayed as Satan knows you no longer are allowing him to play with your heart. Satan knows that he can never be the husband that Jesus is for you and that he falls short of your new husband's power in every situation. The devil in his embarrassment (yes, he is embarrassed he could not continue to play you) and anger, will send so many terrible demons to try to force you away from your husband. These demons will torment you with: guilt, attach desires of lust, cause affliction of disease, horrifying fear, bad memories to bring thoughts of shame, chaotic storms to cause hopelessness, false doctrine to cause confusion, attempt infertility where God wants to birth, cause dysfunction within the family, create division where there is purpose, place strongholds of addiction to decay and will cause finances to slip through your hands like sand. Satan's bruised feelings will put out a high-price bounty to kill everything attached to your new marriage. When these things happen, it is important that you bring it to your husband as He has control of what happens to your marriage.

Jesus is the great conqueror, the unlimited provision, your solid foundation, and the best warrior that will slay every assassin that Satan has sent after you. He can fight for you at maximum capacity when you make His way easy. How do you make your husband's way easy? You must understand your purpose as a bride of Christ. Mathew 5:14-16 says, "You are the light of (Christ to) the world. A city set on a hill cannot be hidden; nor does anyone light a lamp and put it under a basket, but on a lampstand, and it gives light to all who are in the house. Let your light so shine before men in such a way that they may see your good deeds and moral excellence, and (recognize and honor and) glorify your Father who is in Heaven." Understand that you must be a willing vessel to be a light for Christ. This means that obedience is needed when you accept this contract to your husband. Once Christ has placed His light in you, there is nothing that can put this light out. Therefore, you cannot run away from what God has called you to do, and no matter how far you try running away from your calling you cannot stop that action because it has planned destiny. I am a dancer who used to be in Mime ministry, and I sat down in September 2016. Sitting down does not stop me from miming or dancing through gospel music; I do not even realize that I do it because God has placed dance on the inside of me so I cannot control that I move. It did not matter that I chose to sit down from ministry or waste my life being depressed, or that I made excuses that I was stressed out, I still dance even when I do not want to. God has made it a function of who I am because His anointing on it can be used to break chains off the bound. I made the mistake of trying to step in front of what Jesus needed to do, and my mistake had a heavy consequence. Protect the light God has placed in you. Let nothing and no one attempt to harm the purpose within you as your soul is at stake. This is so important because you may be the only representation of God that someone may see.

You can also make Jesus's fight easier by living in service to Him. Do you know a man has enough energy to get through the work of the day when his wife starts his day off with a big meal? I say this because, as a wife, you must learn to feed the Spirit of God that lives inside you. This can be done by starting your day in prayer. Prayer is a tool used to connect and communicate to increase God in your soul. Live a Godly lifestyle and act on decisions the way Jesus would because you know that your husband will be pleased by your actions. Matthew 6:33 says, "But first and most importantly seek (aim at, strive after) His kingdom and His righteousness (His way of doing and being right—the attitude and character of God), and all these things will be given to you also." Victory will be added to you, love will be added to you, power will be added to you, joy will be added to you, peace will be added to you, clarity will be added to you, worth will be added to you, prosperity will be added to you, endurance will be added to you, favor will be added to you, patience will be added to you and you will increase in self-control because you are feeding the Spirit of God in your life.

John 8:31 tells us, "So Jesus was saying to the Jews who had believed Him, 'If you abide in My word (continually obeying My teachings and living in accordance with them, then) you are truly My disciples.'" How can Jesus not honor His word if you trust Him? Always remember when you keep Him first, He will move on your behalf. He will make moves that concern your flesh and grip your emotions because there is a part of it that is about to die. In these moments, trusting God's plan will give peace and healing to your soul even when your flesh is disturbed. Clinging to Jesus will always keep you protected, no matter what happens. There is a victory in flesh disturbance and space for your husband to give you more love. I encourage you to find trust in God because He brings you out victorious in every fight. I encourage you to fight to keep your marriage strong. Love your husband, always take care of his home and tell Him what you need.

Jesus can freely move when you allow Him space to protect what has value to Him. That is right, I said it. Clean up His house! What is His house? "Do you not know that your body is a temple of the Holy Spirit who is within you, whom you have (received as a gift) from God, and that you are not your own (property)? You were bought with a price (you were actually purchased with the precious blood of Jesus and made His own). So then, honor and glorify God with your body." (1 Corinthians 6:19-20) You cannot expect your husband to feel welcome if your house is full of garbage. Realize that garbage is all forms of unclean disorder. I do not want you to be confused, but to breakdown the term garbage that means: lust, fornication, lying, backbiting, manipulation, drug addiction (prescription or not), alcoholism, homosexuality, murdering, suicidal behaviors, racism, malicious attitudes, arrogance, foul language, masturbation, hoarding, abuse, haunting memories, anger, hatred, inappropriate exposure, holding grudges, making excuses, laziness, spreading discourse, attention-grabbing, and violent tendencies.

You were never made to be a trash can because you were purchased with a high price. The price was paid when Jesus's flesh was broken when He took back power, and your husband will not step in and protect or provide for a house that blatantly chooses to live in trash after He has made the ultimate sacrifice for you. Yes, it is so easy to please your flesh, but why stay married to something that would rather kill you if you have access to abundant life? Do not settle for a temporary fix but instead chose to live free. Choose each day to be closer to God, and you will start changing! You are beloved by your husband. Keep up the hard work for your husband because nothing you do goes unnoticed. Your rewards are found in His presence. In this marriage, I know you feel your sacrifice is great but, always remember Jesus sacrificed of everything He had because He knew you were worth going to hell and back.

My Testimony

Skye, lean not to your own understanding! I know when I try to run from God, He always brings me right back to where I belong. My life was never better when I decided it was too hard to live a Godly lifestyle. I tried to go back to shacking up with a man, I wanted to be depressed about a situation I was told to leave, because I had been investing my time and finances in activities that opened doors for hell to come back in my life and I struggled thinking I would never get rid of what I chose to attach myself to.... I saw a sexy man thinking what he had to say was of God and this whole time God was never in his heart. Being so far away from God felt like hell on Earth. I had to stop and say if I never have my stuff returned so what, if I never see another penny returned to me so what! I have to accept that I was at fault and push forward and go with God. It did not take people warning me, it did not take him hurting me, it did not even take me going broke, but it took me choosing to work toward getting back to the will of God to change my mind, to love my first husband before I give myself to another man. If that meant leaving that man alone, I had to do it, if it meant getting out of my bed to spend some time with my children I had to do it, if it meant giving my grocery money to be obedient and bless my parents I had to do it. I must do whatever it takes for however long it takes to manifest because I trust God and I now cling to God.

EVERLASTING

"Jesus Christ is (eternally changeless, always) the same yesterday and today and forever." (Hebrews 13:8) I am so thankful God is everlasting! He is always present, and you can take joy and pleasure in knowing that there is no end to God. We are going to review how having access to an everlasting God benefits you since we know that man has an expected end. What does Jesus being changeless do for you on your journey in life?

In Revelations 22:13, God says that He is Alpha and Omega, which means that He is the beginning and the end. God has always been in control, no matter what or who comes and goes throughout life. This means that God gave you purpose before life; since He honors His word, He will be there for you until there is an end. Understand clearly that Jesus stays with you in the process of your journey through life. God is always going to be present in every situation you encounter. When trouble presents itself know that God is there, when you think you are alone, know that God is there, when you are contemplating the unimaginable know that God is there, when you are struggling know that God is there, when you feel confused or hopeless know that God is there, and even when your life may seem perfect, know that God is there with you. Some people forget that God's favor is the only reason life may run well. I know Jesus to be an uplifting force no matter what we are going through when I found truth in Matthews 14:22-33, in the familiar story of

Jesus walking on water. There are so many great points hidden in this passage to prove the present of God never ceases.

Many people have not analyzed this story for the valuable lesson it teaches or else the world would be calmer. Jesus sent the disciples out before Him, so they were obedient and piled into the boat. This means that when God sends you that you have been activated with authority and sent forth to complete your assignment. This is God saying you are being released with purpose. Then there was a great storm, and there was panic that arose in the boat among the disciples. There should have never been panic or chaos because God was there with them in the storm. When you are on assignment, you will be presented with challenges because what needs to be done is great, and the enemy does not want you to be successful. Since God has control of the enemy, He will allow these things to happen to see if you stay obedient to His calling. What are you tripping on in your storm? See the disciples knew of God but were not strong enough in their faith (to trust God), or else they would have remembered God's will is what will always be done, and if it were God's will the ship would have splintered. In these trials is not where you give up, but where you push through until God says it's done. If it is God's will then you might as well thank Him for keeping you in every storm because He could have let you die while the sky became clouded, the rain fell, and the waves swelled. You could have died dealing with your problems, but God's hand was on your ship, and He did not allow you to go under.

God sent His son as a reminder to the disciples of His power and protection. God sent Jesus to you to remind you that you are being kept safe in the storm because you are valued to His kingdom. That is why you saw people dropping dead dealing with the same addiction, and God spared you to make the deliverance from your addiction a testimony. In the story, Jesus is walking toward the boat to reveal the purpose and show power, and Satan saw what was about to happen. Remember that worry and doubt, the panic and chaos are emotional forms of demonic action. "I don't know God if I can make it!" God did not doubt your ability to weather the storm and reach your destination or else He would have never sent you. The storm is the distraction to misguide you away from purpose. God is in the midst of it all waiting to see if you are going to move on emotion or stand in faith. At this point in the story, the disciples were confused, and when they saw Jesus, they assumed death was coming for them. Jesus is on the way to meet you in your situation when it feels like you will be consumed by death. Truly, it is amazing to have seen the miraculous and still not trust God. Even when Jesus came forward, He was still questioned, as the rest of the disciples were too afraid to approach Jesus. Why in the middle of hell draping us do we question if God will ever step in and save us from assumed danger? It happens when we look at the trouble around us and become focused on what we see instead of remembering what we know and stand on those facts. Our storms could be anything that will distract us, and at that moment, we need to pray.

Trust not what you see or what your flesh feels but trust God in the middle of absolute chaos. What we do know is that God is greater than our storm and it is important to call on God to guide us and sustain us even when we fear and are no longer in a place of peace. Stay strong in God's word and declare it to the storm; keep it in the forefront of every action taken during the storm because our faith is being tested. If you make a mistake repent whole-heartedly and move forward if you fall get back up and move forward. The disciples failed their test, and God sent Jesus to them to give a physical representation to the disciples of His presence. It was Peter who questioned Jesus to be God's presence in chaos. This speaks volumes as we know the importance of Peter to the church, and even he still wanted to be sure that God was God. Peter said, 'Lord bring me to You if You are standing out on the sea.' Do not wait to see Jesus or to question God to the point He must send someone to bring peace. Draw near to God for yourself and see that no matter how long the storm, that you will be pushed to a place of peace.

The other important benefit of God being everlasting is that God will never change who He is in your life, and His will always functions according to His Word. "The grass withers, the flower fades, but the word of our God stands forever." (Isaiah 40:8) Reading the Bible in its entirety, you will never find loopholes for sin to enter into God's plans and reign in that situation. This means that you cannot change the Word or omit pieces of scripture to fit God around your plans. This is awesome because human nature (fleshly desire) is clouded and will always fail, but what is done through God will stand. God cannot change His mind or omit to cover you in the storm. Our fleshly nature will regret decisions, move out of anger, and change our minds to act with malice toward what we assume is an enemy. God can send Jesus to walk out to grab you and pull you close to Him when you crept too far out of faith and are drowning in a sea of your mistakes. Proverbs 14:12 tells us that if we act on our ways what we have put into action will fail, so God analyzes what is prayed for and sees what the impact of answered prayers are to His kingdom. This makes sense when you pray for a house and are upset that it was not received because God knew it was not going to be fit for you and saw what was going to happen in that house. I prayed for a house; God was not going to release it to me because I would not keep my apartment clean. God changed my heart and my situation, which was better than any prayer I had prayed before this change. God gave me insight that Jesus is here to catch me when mistakes are made and my responsibility was to learn from my mistakes so that they are not repeated.

It is important to have God leading every decision. Choose to let God lead you no matter what your situation may be and remember not to allow it to distract you from what God has told you to do. I encourage you to stand on God and complete your assignment. Remember that the greater the storm, the bigger the mission and the better the reward of completing your assignment. Just when you are ready to move in fear, be at peace and remember God has you covered, and He is in control. God has spoken completion to your storm! God has put an expiration date on the problems that afflict you so be encouraged to weather the storm.

My Testimony

It was heavy in my heart when writing this section of the book that I had to stop acting on emotion. I began reading in Matthews and realized that Jesus never had to walk on water. This hit me in the face hard. Jesus had to walk out because of assumed danger. I sat there and vowed not to let any situation I am experiencing be bigger than my prayer life to God, and whatever happens, God's will is working on my behalf. The next morning this was tested by God with a loss of something that I let sway my emotions. And I stood and said, "God, I will stay right here, and I let you heal me, and this is working for my good!" I had peace. I picked myself up and went to make my kids breakfast. I stopped worrying about what could happen or being upset about what I lost and could no longer pout about my situation. I saw that it was foolish to be worked up about my storm because God was in control and even if I do not understand it in my storm, everything I am facing will work for my good. I had to stand through slander, humiliation, exile, debt, and losing what I love the most not knowing that I would be tormented and made a laughing stalk to the very people I thought cared. He kept me at peace, and since this incident may affect me for years, I am okay knowing God is still in control, and God's vengeance on my enemies is worse than anything I could imagine. I had to keep rehearsing His word and it kept me from retaliating because my actions would have made the words of these liars true. My rebellious nature rose and I looked in the mirror daily and said, "I refuse to quit, I will not die, I refuse to give up this time."

FORGIVENESS

God designed this section of the manual to speak about the benefits and empowerment that comes with forgiving others. He says that it is also imperative that you understand and fully comprehend the consequences that come with unforgiveness and how spiritually hoarding guilt and the thoughts that weigh are canceling spiritual growth. Understand that forgiving and pardoning others allows God to forgive you of the sins you have committed. "If we freely admit that we have sinned and confess our sins, He is faithful and just, true to His own nature and promises, and will forgive our sins and cleanse us continually from all unrighteousness our wrongdoing, everything not in conformity with His will and purpose." (1 John 1:9) What this is saying is that God is a God of second chances. He understands the condition of our flesh and gives us new opportunities to repent and ask for forgiveness. The Word also says God is true to His nature because He can bless what is like Him. I love that He promised to continually wash and purge us of wrongdoing, meaning that God continually gives us chances to live in His will, which is the way He intended. Forgiveness is for everyone, and to forgive is an essential part of our spiritual growth in the Lord. Forgiveness is a constant that is vital to our lives and must be practiced every day all day.

We know that forgiveness is important, so when do we start working on forgiving others? To answer this question, know that forgiving others starts with you making a change first. Mark 11:25

says, "Whenever you stand praying, if you have anything against anyone, forgive him, drop the issue, let it go, so that your Father who is in heaven will also forgive you your transgressions and wrongdoings against Him and others." Prayer is the perfect time to deal with unforgiveness. I recommend that you do this, especially if you know that your attitude is confrontational because it allows you to have time to confess the real problem within you that does not allow you to forgive the person that hurt you. Because forgiveness is for you and God must heal your heart first, be open and truthful to the Lord as the truth will make you free. Pray about the walls that are building between you and that person and why God wants to use them in your life. Pray for the change to happen within your own heart, as it will take prayer to release you from the pain that causes you not to forgive. Once you start praying, you will have some questions come to mind.

You might be asking, "How often should I forgive those who sin against me?" Peter had the same question, and when he asked Jesus, the answer was given. In Matthew 18:22, Jesus replied, "I say to you, not up to seven times, but seventy times seven." Unfortunately, this is taken literal, but Jesus wanted there to be a deeper revelation to the frequency of forgiving others. He is saying is that forgiveness needs to be made as a habit until our character is changed. People sin every day, and it is important that we understand we are going to mess up because imperfection is a condition of our flesh. On an average day, a person makes 35,000 choices, not all of them perfect, so this means that continually pardoning others for their wrongdoings should be a choice made all day. Establish habitual forgiveness as a core concept of your character as it shows that you have strength and Godly expectations of others.

You might also ask, "Why is showing compassion and forgiveness important to my walk in faith?" Forgiveness brings many benefits for you as it allows God's love will shine deeper in you, making His presence in you radiant to everyone. A massive benefit forgiveness brings is healing. 2 Corinthians 2:7 tells us that instead of further rebuking those who caused us pain, we should graciously forgive, comfort and encourage them to keep them from being overwhelmed by sorrow. First, recognize that the people who are hurting you are hurting within themselves. Yes, their soul is messed up and will tend to act on emotion which they usually regret. Second, realize the concept of graciously forgiving and what it means to forgive with grace. This hit me hard because it took me a long time to understand how to forgive people who hurt me graciously. My downfall was that I loved those who hurt me, like family and friends. I internalized what was happening or what had already happened to me in an attempt to avoid being offensive or lashing out from the pain it caused. Graciously forgiving had to be practiced continually to be mastered, because this is lovingly forgiving, loving pardoning and knowing that what was happening was exposing the mess within myself. I will speak further about this in the next section. Third, now that we know that this person is lashing out from their own pain, we need to comfort them. We remember why compassion is so important and must be shown as those who are hurting may be experiencing labor pains.

Forgiving means that you must uplift the hurting to the Lord and ask for their pain to be released and that they are pardoned from every wrongdoing they have committed. Compassionate care for the hurting allows blessings of a healing atmosphere. Bring encouragement by speaking life into this hurting person. Remember that God tells us in Hebrews 12:14, to make peace with everyone. Forgiving without respecter of person helps with making peace. Everyone means just that – because you are not sent just to love the "Feel Good" bunch. It is so easy to get caught up in loving those who have your best interest at heart, pat you on the back for accomplishments or those who motivate you to keep moving toward success, but they are a select group of people who you are required to make peace with in life. Everyone stretches to your haters, backstabbers, downers, bad influences, irritators, aggressors, cheaters, drainers, those who wish harm against you, those who have wounded you, those who reject your Godly character and every enemy that presents itself. Look past the faults of others because they are not a problem, but a test God has put you through to see if you are going to display holy behavior and allow Him to be glorified amid problems. Jesus Christ understood the importance of forgiveness. I say this because Jesus asked God to forgive us because we did not understand the magnitude of our actions. Jesus who was spit on, beaten unrecognizably, made to bear his casket (cross) and mocked still knew we needed deliverance. He understood that after all we put Him through that God needed to be put away from anger against us and allow the prophecy to be fulfilled. Despite the pain He suffered, He was willing to go through it to continually ask for forgiveness on our behalf.

Forgiveness has the benefit of bringing deliverance from strongholds in your life. Strongholds are your own mental hang-ups you think about that are holding you down and holding you back. Strongholds are the conceptions of Satan attempting to validate to you and defend the lies he created for you about your life so that you believe what he is saying is a part of your being. So many people choose to rehearse their past and use it to keep blaming someone for their problems. This is an attack from Satan because he knows that when you are stuck in the past, you will not step into your future. Satan knows if you are weighed down, you have the opportunity to drown. When operating with forgiveness, there must be an acceptance of having the mind of Christ. Jesus Christ loves and forgives you; in Christ-like thinking, you find unconditional love, forgiveness, inner peace, and freedom. Once you are forgiven, that sin was cast into the Sea of Forgetfulness because that weight will have to drown on its own. Letting go of the past makes your mind free of negativity and destructive behavior, and free to move forward with purpose. Forgiving your past, the father who abandoned you, the boyfriend or girlfriend who broke your heart, the bully who told you that you would never be worth anything, the family that planted lies against your great potential to be successful and every lie to assassinate who you are in God, it allows you to be free of these forms of destruction. You have now decided to turn forward to walk into your purpose as you are choosing not to be bound by your past.

You will also flourish in the benefit of humility when you act with forgiveness. I studied humility and found in reading Luke

6:31-37 that anyone can grasp the meaning of being humble. This goes back to when I spoke about making peace with everyone. It is important to grasp that loving and caring for those who are a part of our inner circle or comfortable relationships still defeats the blessing of forgiveness. We are taught this lesson as children, especially when we have that one person we cannot get along with on the playground. Why are we then missing the Golden Rule as adults? We as adults want to take control of our lives and feel that we do not need to submit to rules that govern our attitudes. Life is lived some much in a state of "I" that the concept of appropriate, responsible, and loving communication has ceased. The Golden Rule exists because there are rules that give a distinction between unholy and holy living. The Word tells us that forgiveness to pleasant relationships profits us nothing because it is an action that even ungodly people understand can be done. When we function in the ways of God, we want nothing less than the best outcome, the best life, abundant life for all of mankind. Mastering forgiveness releases blessings in our favor because we have the understanding to act without emotion and act with Godly behavior.

Looking through the scriptures, we have established that forgiveness is a choice, so is unforgiveness. When you choose not to forgive, you are holding too much in your soul. Unforgiveness is overbearing, spiritual hoarding! With hoarding, people become so full of negativity that it embodies their actions and behavior. Holding on to hatred for your rapist or molester because they have attached identity confusion to you is weighing you down. Bringing your feelings about your past five relationships into your new one is causing division. Holding on to the past pain, hoarding hatred against your abuser is eating love out of your soul. Holding conversations with the multiple personalities you have created that are encouraging you to act deadly cloud your heart with evil intentions. Hoarding unforgiveness from other people and spreading your pain by gossiping against the person who hurt you just to have someone share in your hatred. Taking drugs as a way of avoiding or rejecting pain is causing disease to rot you away inside and shorten your life. Unforgiveness is such emotional baggage. Imagine carrying bags of groceries. These bags represent the space in your heart. Think of what you have in your heart and that it is harder to carry negativity than carrying positive feelings. What are you holding in your bags? Is it bitterness, gossip, self-servicing pleasure, backbiting, anger, regret, doubt, joy, love, peace, etc.? What are you really allowing into your heart?

How can God pour into you His blessings if you are already full of bitterness, resentment, jealousy, envy, or hatred? This personal issue must be resolved to express the expectations of God. I had to start praying that God gives me the strength because at one point, I was full of garbage, and I wanted to keep holding on to my garbage. I did not understand how to release garbage until I changed my mindset. I started praying because I saw that I was naïve, thinking about this person being an enemy, and they end up being a blessing in my life. I realized if God could use rocks to praise, He could use anyone to fix and deal with my issues. I have to fight to look past what I see on the surface because that person may have an encouraging word to give me, they may have a testimony that tells me to hold on and stay strong, they could be waiting to help me get a breakthrough, and they may be an angel in disguise waiting to release a blessing. God added wisdom, and now I try to remember that I could hold on to something that is creating death in my life or let it go so that God can pour into my soul. He allowed me to realize that unforgiveness and being merciless hold up the greatness of God and that this attitude prevents us from moving forward in life with purpose. If garbage is held, you can become clouded with death in your spirit, your heart is hardened, and it will start to manifest in the body in ways of disease, illness and several disruptions of function.

I encourage you to stand open, praying, being humble, and forgiving others. I encourage you to live with purpose. I encourage you to allow God to mend your heart so that you may find acceptance and forgiveness. And, when you slip or get angry, I encourage you to pray that you let go of the choice you made to be mad and live life abundantly happy.

My Testimony

I learned the hard way that forgiveness is needed for healing. I held so much hatred for years that it was killing the God in me. I mean, I was mad at people who could care less about how I felt and enjoying their lives; sleeping peacefully. I had held on to so much hate that I would talk to myself in my head (yes I held conversations like that person was there) about how I would tell someone off about hurting my kids' feelings, treating me terrible and how I would deny someone who uses me the next time they ask for my help. I was fine telling my pastor that I felt no compassion for anyone, and that life is life dealt with it when it happens. How stupid was that? Skye, you could have been playing with your kids, Skye you could have been smiling, you could have kept your mind on God and not thought about placing your own wrath in that situation. I looked back and realized my mind was in a terrible place that I could see someone telling me off, and thoughts of stabbing them entered my head. I started to think about what I would not take and what violence I wanted to inflict in its place. I was hurt deep.

When I started this section, it was to be about faith, and God told me to change it. He said that I have a full understanding of His word, but I have held on to so much trash and negativity that I am missing so much of my purpose. I began to get in the scriptures, and I wept. I cried and cried and cried. How could I expect God to forgive me of my faults if I could not forgive someone who hurt my feelings? God, I promised to let you use me, and I know I must change my life. Every day is a process, I am getting better at letting it go, and soon this temple will be empty of all trash! Every day I feel better because I do not have to rehearse in my mind so much anger, and I am happier; I am closer to God. I see a drastic change in how I treat my children and how I approach life. I slip some days, but I pray that God when I can't let go of the problem that He take it from me as I find a way never to pick up and dwell on that issue again. Lord, I would rather be free from multiple personalities; I would rather fill my bags with love, or even leave some open and empty to be able to receive from the Lord than take a choice of cancer and poison.

GRACE

Grace, in its simplest form, is unmerited favor.

As physical beings, we sin, and our sins can leave us in positions where we should not be warranted any favor from God. "For it is by grace (God's remarkable compassion and favor drawing you to Christ) that you have been saved (actually delivered from judgment and given eternal life) through faith. And this (salvation) is not of yourselves (not through your own effort), but it is the (undeserved, gracious) gift of God; not as a result of your works (nor your attempts to keep the Law), so that no one will (be able to) boast or take credit in any way (for his salvation)." (Ephesians 2:8-9) Grace mainly exists to allow God to bless us as His children when we are still in sin.

Many of us are aware that there are some things we have right now, that if man made the decision, we would never possess, but by God's grace we were still allowed to receive these gifts. Many of us can look back at our lives and find that God's grace was present when He made a way of escape from Satan's grip that tried to kill us or have us locked up for life. In this section, we will have the opportunity to study the value of God's grace and the power it holds.

I wanted to start by saying that there is so much blessing to partake in simply by being an obedient child of God. Yes, your obedience will allow God to move with unmerited favor on your behalf when you make a mistake.

One of the best people to prove this type of grace was David.

Many of us know David to be the slayer of beasts, defeater of giants and a king. Many do not read that David also had issues with lust and adultery. One of the best stories of David's issues with lust and God's grace is found in 2 Samuel 11-12. David's desires got the best of him one day when he walked out on his roof and saw Bathsheba taking a bath. It was in this moment he slipped because he desired to sleep with this beautiful woman even when he was informed that she was married, and David still decided to have sex with Bathsheba. David attempted to hide what he did in lust, so he sent his general out and ended up killing Bathsheba's husband when David's original plan of deception fell apart.

Notice that David's sin and mistake did not cause David to lose his position as king, even in the denial of his treacherous actions. God still knew David's actions when David thought he could lie and deny in this situation, and he was still forgiven. David was finally confronted by God, he repented and to spare David's life, God killed David and Bathsheba's baby.

David's mistake tells us that our flesh will always have areas of weakness. God knows that we have fleshly desires, and He does not have an unrealistic expectation that we will never fall or make moves that will please our flesh. For example, God knows what I did when I stepped down from ministry, and no matter what I told others and myself He knew my flesh was weak. God still picked me up and reaccepted me back, and it came with a price. God will step in to fix our mistakes, but His grace comes with a price. Thankfully, God knew David's heart, and the blessings God had in store for him were kept long after David's life had ended.

David's situation also proved that God's warnings would always come before the decision is made to move out of weakness. When we have a true relationship with God, He has a way of convicting us when we make a poor choice. God will still allow multiple chances for us to repent from our mistakes. Remember that God is a loving father, and we find this in His Word in Ephesians 4:32. This tells us that repentance and forgiveness are needed so that we do not continue to live in sin, but that we learn to resist worldly desires. This is the core concept of unmerited favor. God sat and waited to give time to David to acknowledge and be responsible to repent about his inappropriate behavior. This tells us that when we have a purpose to His kingdom, God's forgiveness and grace can switch what could have hurt us to be a testimony to save someone else.

Grace saves us from hellacious suffering, but we must not forget that there are consequences for our actions, and someone must answer when our full sin is revealed. David's repentance allowed his son to die because of grace. When we have a sin that we have benefitted from, we can expect grace to cut it off, and that assumed blessing will die. This is a death that must happen so that the result will be a healthy life that will flourish in God's will. This would be like stealing money to buy a car, you repent for stealing the money, and the car is totaled soon after the confession of your sin. God's grace will not abound in the riches of sin, and all the sin attached to what you need grace to abolish must be cut down. God's grace will keep His blessings and promises to you and your bloodline because God will still bless you when you work to have the will of God be fulfilled.

God's grace was also designed to show His triumphant power. If we fight and fall while being tested, it does not show God is victorious. However, the raising and the conquering in areas of failure show that God will give the grace to restore. I found proof of triumphant grace in 1 Peter 5:10 which states, "After you have suffered for a little while, the God of all grace (who imparts His blessing and favor), who called you to His own eternal glory in Christ, will Himself complete, confirm, strengthen, and establish you (making you what you ought to be)." This told me that some suffering is not for us to handle, and sometimes we must suffer to be granted triumphant grace. Our suffering is the problem or problems we face when we choose to serve God wholeheartedly. Suffering allows us to be humble and is a part of us walking Christ-like. Our suffering is a requirement for grace to be shown as a testimony of His victory and His power. It is here, in this suffering, being humiliated and our character, values, and faith being mocked and persecuted, where God will bless us in front of our enemies. I have enough moments of triumphant grace that it encourages me that I am headed in the right direction toward more purpose and more power. See the suffering I am meant to handle results in an increase. When we go through hard trials, there tends to be a resilience towards the enemy's tricks. For example, when someone keeps pushing your buttons, you eventually stop cursing about it and you start praying about the situation. Then when you see that person again, you greet them with unconditional love and create the bond that Satan tried to destroy. This type of suffering brings completion to the problem you are facing. Remind yourself that your storm, this present chaos, this present wounding, this present pain has an expected end because God declares that it will be complete! God already spoke that this suffering would establish you, which means that you will be secured and anchored where you need to be to do the works of the Lord! This also means that God is not required to grant grace to someone who is not in His will.

Remember unmerited favor by God is granted to those who are abiding in holy living. If someone chooses to be ineffective to the Kingdom of God, there is no reason for God to give them power because it will not be used. Do not be confused about ineffective living or point the finger at someone when you need to check to make sure you are living holy. It does you no good to create a hierarchy of sin when sin is sin, period. If you are willfully sinning, you are ineffective to the Kingdom. If you are not in prayer and communing with God, you are ineffective to the Kingdom. If you only read God's Word at face value but never seek revelation, you are ineffective to the Kingdom. If you are not doing as God tells you because you feel like making excuses instead of trusting God for strength, you too are ineffective to the Kingdom. Ineffective living causes unnecessary struggles that God never intended us to go through. For example, if I do not pay my tithes and offerings after I have attended a five-week Bible study on the value of giving, I have chosen not just to live ineffectively but to live without funds that God cannot release to me amid my disobedience. I encourage you to live effectively because it is vital if you plan on living an abundant life. An abundant life is not an easy life, but it is a blessed life. Effective living will cause God to release generational blessing and the opportunity to see miracles, signs, and wonders in your own life. I encourage you to live a fact-based life and not move out of feelings that could cause you to miss the blessings of triumphant grace!

My Testimony

The grace of God is real in my life, and therefore no one can change my mind about the existence and presence of God.

God's saving grace has shown favor in so many areas of my life because I know I have made enough failed suicide attempts, blatantly enjoyed sinning even though I am a minister, willfully spoke death when I felt praying was going to be ineffective, sat down on my calling, wasted tons of money, enjoyed deadly addictions and I am still alive because of grace.

I know that the fact that I am still breathing free and not serving any sentences in prison is by the grace of God. The fact God still gave me words to write while setting this book down on multiple occasions is God's grace. I have been taken through so much suffering that my full testimony cannot fit here in this short space. It has caused me to find my purpose as an encourager and to live as a testimony of what God can birth in you to make you an overcomer!

REFERENCE SCRIPTURES

 AWAKENING
- Ephesians 5:13-14
- John 15:16
- James 1:8
- Genesis 2:1

 BLESSINGS
- Proverbs 10:3; 10:6; 28:20
- Ephesians 1:3-5
- John 10:28

 COMPASSION
- 1 John 3:18
- Hebrews 13:1-3
- Galatians 6:2
- Matthews 9:36-38

 DISCIPLESHIP
- Ephesians 5:23-24
- Mathew 5:14-16; 6:33
- John 8:31
- 1 Corinthians 6:19-20

 EVERLASTING
- Hebrews 13:8
- Revelations 22:13
- Matthews 14:22-33
- Isiah 40:8
- Proverbs 14:12

 FORGIVENESS
- 1 John 1:9
- Matthew 18:22
- 2 Corinthians 2:7
- Mark 11:25
- Hebrews 12:14
- Luke 6:31-37

 GRACE
- Ephesians 2:8-9; 4:32
- 2 Samuel 11-12
- 1 Peter 5:10

Book Sponsors

1. Philippa Lee: Miracles work in very small ways and in God's time. I encourage you to read this book for your miracle is waiting!

2. CrowdPublish.Tv: visit http://CrowdPublish.TV for livestreamed Conversations to make you Think & take Action!

3. Jaime Sanborn: My friend, my sister from another mister. I love you and am so proud of you and how far you have come. You are one of the most generous people I have ever known. May God continue to bless you and your boys as you have been a blessing to my family. Thank you for all that you do and who you are. You'll always have a sister in me. Congratulations on your book!

4. Derek Decamp: You have to have faith in yourself before anyone else will have faith in you.

Apostle Kelvin Hines

Prophetess Audra Hines

Service Times
Sunday Worship Service 10 a.m
Tuesday Night Impact Bible Study 7 p.m

Abundant Life World Ministries
1914 E. Roeser Road, Phoenix, Arizona

Printed in the United States
By Bookmasters